10 Little Rules
for
Your
Creative Soul

by Rita Long
with Carol Pearson

DEDICATION

Dedicated to my Mother and Father...
who both, in their own different ways, told me
"You can do whatever you want to do."

CONTENTS

ACKNOWLEDGMENTS

Being supported shows up in my life in so many ways.

Carol Pearson turns words into symphonies and gently nudged me until I believed I could actually write a book. My sisters, Barbara and Rosemary, have always supported my uniqueness and are the most loyal "big sisters" possible.

My son Ryan and my daughter Kristin embrace my creativity and stand strong in their own truth and individuality. On the home front, my husband Doug is always willing to watch me spread my wings and sometimes dance on peanut butter, all the while smiling. Cherished friends and precious grandchildren fill my life bubble with joy.

I have a "Spiritual Board of Directors" (both passed and alive) who lend me their wisdom and insights through books, lectures and conversation. And when I really, really need healing I go to the Sea. She lifts me up and grounds me all at the same time.

Sat - Chit – Ananda
Always Shine Your Light!

FOREWORD
by Carol Pearson

Sometimes it's the things that wreck us, those moments that bring us to our knees, that make way for what's next in our lives and make us whole. So it was with me several years ago, when I found myself facing a life that I didn't recognize as my own.

After much reflection and soul searching, I realized that I'd been living my life according to everyone's rules but my own. It was time to rebuild my life. Out of that process was born "10 Little Rules for a Blissy Life," the first in our series of 10 Little Rules books.

A few years later I met Rita Long, and was immediately pulled into her vortex of light and creativity. The way she explored life and lived her own rules was a perfect fit to the 10 Little Rules, and this book that you're reading was the outcome of our friendship and our shared journey toward a more creative and fulfilling life, both personally and professionally.

Partnering with Rita to bring this book into existence has been a brilliant challenge and a process of pure joy. I hope you'll enjoy it and take away what you need to go out and live a more creative, more blissy and more joy-filled life.

"Creative Living is living a life
that is driven more strongly
by curiosity than by fear."

Elizabeth Gilbert
in *Big Magic*

INTRODUCTION – YOUR CREATIVE LIFE

I was an artist, in my mind, when I was 8 years old. Where it came from I don't know, but I found myself sketching and longing to take an art class. There were no art classes available to me, and "being an artist" was foreign to my family and my situation. So I just drew sometimes…because it felt good. Meanwhile I married, had children, worked, started my own business and retired without doing any art.

Only when I retired did I start to paint. One day, while missing the involvement, learning and growth that my career had given me, I found myself in a store buying all the art supplies I could lay my hands on and setting up a studio in a large corner of a bathroom in my home. Yes, I said bathroom.

I entered another universe. Not being a "laugh out loud" kind of person, I found myself gently giggling in the middle of the night when I stood back and realized my painting was actually not bad, and I had a sense of joy running through my veins again. I call this the "Yummy Giggles" – that feeling that reflects a peaceful truth that has found its home inside you.

I live an artful and creative life…I want everything I do to be full of passion and bliss…my choices, my challenges, my companions, my rewards, my home, my conversations, my work, my experiences, my everything.

If you are reading this book, this much must be true for you: On some level, you believe that you are creative, or at the very least have the ability to live a more creative and artful life, if only you can figure out what that means.

There is a reason this book landed in your hands at exactly this time. Any self-limiting beliefs you hold onto will shape your life. If you truly believed you aren't a creative person, you would not be reading this book. Instead there is something deep, deep inside you, in that part that is not your mind or brain, which is seeking more fulfillment and growth. I wholeheartedly believe that being creative is our way of seeking self-expression…and that self-expression takes form in many ways besides what we traditionally call "art."

Where does it start? Where does it come from? Read on, soul seekers.

I look back on that small child, long ago, longing to draw and paint…in a world where no one she knew was an artist and those kinds of dreams were not understood. Her small, solitary efforts were eventually pushed aside by the more practical principles needed to travel through life.

I learned to navigate through life in a respectable and successful manner, yet the yearning to be more creative was always simmering at the base of my spine and in the bottom of my heart. Little did I know that I could have done this years before if I had known one important truth about creativity and the role it would play in my life.

That truth? It's so simple. I. AM. CREATIVE. Period.

I now acknowledge and honor that truth as part of my being. I could have done this all along, but the idea of being creative in corporate America isn't always a priority and in fact, is often discouraged. Looking back, I was dramatically creative in the way I taught adult education. Most of my students agreed. Yet there was this real (or imagined?) bubble that many times locked in my desire to express myself, grow, create and share. It felt like I was wearing invisible handcuffs.

How do I know this? Every time I made the decision to change, in any way, it was preceded by feelings of either sadness, physical pain (usually in my gut), hopelessness, fear, worry and the paralysis of analysis because I questioned my own "inner knower" when it guided me to do something other than what was the "normal" thing to do.

Not trusting my inner knower made me physically ill. It's crazy. Why do we trust others more than ourselves? For a fantastic explanation of this idea of the "inner knower," go to YouTube and watch Steven Spielberg's talk "Listen to the Whispers." It will help you understand that you already have the answers you need to walk your own path of creativity, if you only take the time to be quiet and listen. Respect The Whispers!

So yes, I am creative. And so are you. We all are. The proof of this exists all around us. Look around and see what you have created so far – the way you've decorated your home; what you prepared for lunch; the relationships you've built. Was it by default or by conscious intention? Did you just get lucky? Or did you tap into something big and bold with certainty and clarity? Maybe you have an inner knowing about what you want to create, but are waiting for the right time, the right teacher, and the right signs to set you on your creativity journey. Or maybe you don't yet trust your own creative instincts, looking to others to help you decide what your life will look like.

We create our lives, minute by minute, every moment of the day. Some do it unconsciously, never stopping to realize that yes; this life is indeed of their making. These are the ones who pine for things to be another way or yearn for more freedom to express. Others, the ones we call "creative" for how they express themselves in their careers or their entire lives, choose to consciously create their lives.

Say it out loud….I. AM CREATIVE. Living a more creative life starts with this one truth. Own it, and make an intention right now to acknowledge this as part of your life and your being. You deserve it. And when you hear whisperings of creative want, no matter how soft, small or timid, recognize that this is your truth trying to get your attention. If we ignore the whispers, the cosmic 2x4 will visit, and that is not fun!

Creativity is not a gift bestowed on just a select few. Creativity is not sacred. We are all creative, and we create all the time. The magic begins when we listen to those murmurings and make the choice to do something about them.

Research on creativity proves that being creative is rarely a singular act or idea, but rather one of many. "As strange as it sounds, creativity can become a habit," says creativity researcher Jonathan Plucker, PhD, a psychology professor at Indiana University.[1] "Making it one helps you become more productive." The idea that turns into creative expression is chosen, nurtured and given wings. While scientists attempt to explain where creativity comes from, philosophers have long written about our deep human instinct to create.

The beauty of creativity is that you don't have to understand it on a scholarly level to practice it. It's waiting for you. It's already there, calling your name. Listen. It's Inspiration, Intuition, Awareness, Ideas, Consciousness, Images — it's asking you to go for a ride, begging "Pick me! Pick Me!" Are we listening, or are we second guessing or ignoring those creative urges?

Jack Canfield, the co-author of "Chicken Soup for the Soul," talks about "planned action" versus "soul-inspired action." Planned action is relatively easy for us; we do it all the time. We figure out "how" to live the life we have decided we want, we set goals, make to-do lists and move toward our next step. Soul-inspired action, on the other hand, comes to us either like a bolt of lightning or a gentle whisper, but it's strong, powerful and persistent.

As Canfield writes, "Your subconscious mind is the source of your hidden genius and will always provide you with the knowledge you need to move forward in the right direction. This is true for all people, not just those who consider themselves to be psychic or highly intuitive."[2]

To me it's like the scent of jasmine on an evening walk through a garden: You're not sure where it's coming from but it's all around you and it lingers, touching some spark of awareness deep inside. That's the spark of your creative power. That's your creative intuition asking you to go for that ride, like a child asking the parent to play and have fun.

The next time you feel this inspiration, whisper, intuition, awareness or creative instinct, say YES! Just go for the ride. See where it takes you. Try a version of it on, like a warm winter coat on a cold day. If it doesn't fit you can always take it off.

Choosing to live a more creative life can be daunting. I know; I've slogged through the transition that at times felt overwhelming. These 10 Little Rules have helped me break through the storm of uncertainty and fear to a place of creative clarity. My hope is that they will help you too. I recommend you read through the book, do the exercise at the end of each chapter, and then take some time to reflect and ask yourself "what can I do today" to start your ride to a more creative, more magical life. For it truly is magical. And yes, we are all afraid to step outside our comfort zones. Don't worry about that. Feel the fear, and then do it anyway.

Now is your moment. Now is your chance to take control and start living that life that more fully honors your creative soul. Of course, it's important to remember that these rules work for me; they may not be right for you, and I'm not offering any advice on how to live your life, only sharing with you what has worked – like magic – for me. You may find you create an entirely different set of rules for yourself. Let's take this journey together, with love and a wide open heart. And lots of yummy giggles.

You'll notice that at the end of each chapter is plenty of space for your notes, thoughts, doodles or musings. We encourage you to make this book your own testament to your creative life, however that looks to you. Enjoy.

Rita Long with Carol Pearson

"Embrace silence since meditation
is the only way to truly come
to know your Source."

Dr. Wayne W. Dyer

RULE #1 – THOU SHALT NOT STEAL

Most of us are raised to have high regard for this ethical rule in our everyday life. We know it's wrong to steal. Yet we steal from ourselves all the time, and seem unwilling or unable to recognize it when it's happening on a personal level. We steal from our creative power source every time we make a decision to do for others at the expense of doing for ourselves.

I don't believe we do this on purpose. Instead, I believe it happens because we are trying so hard to do what's right, that we often neglect to listen to what we need to feel fulfilled. In our world of instant gratification and multi-tasking, how can we possibly know what we truly want? Or why? As Carol Pearson said in her first book in this series, "10 Little Rules for a Blissy Life," our hearts would have to scream to be heard over all the noise in our daily lives.

The constant doing, thinking, arranging, orchestrating, planning, and texting create barriers to our bliss. We seem to hear everyone and everything except ourselves. If we are not allowing ourselves the necessity of silence each day, how we really feel is out of our control. We give our power away. We steal from our own precious creative source.

There is a silent space that only you can access. And no one is going to make that space for you; we must create that space for ourselves. Finding that silent space opens you to unexplained feelings, insights and understandings. If we want to live a more creative life, we must find a way to go to that silent space **regularly**. We must get off the Brain Train, and onto our Soul Train. Your alone time is just as, and quite possibly more, important as the time you spend with others.

Knowing something intellectually and putting it into practice are two wildly different things. One recent morning I grabbed my coffee and went into my studio. But I didn't paint. I looked at my calendar, first thing, to see all the commitments I had to other people that day. The doctor, the grandson's ballgame, the groceries, the party, the emails to answer, the marketing, the plumber; I asked myself an important question. "Where is Rita on this calendar?"

Then and there, I cleared a corner of a back room and asked my hubby to help me move a loveseat in there. Bingo! I added a dim, soft lamp that was stored away and created my sanctuary. Now that space is my first stop each morning. Sometimes I just sit there, other times I meditate or listen to music. The only constant is the quiet.

If we truly aspire to be more creative, we have to sit in silence and ask ourselves really good questions. "Why am I so fat?" is not a good question. It does nothing to help. "Why do I always screw this up" is also not helpful. "Who am I?" or "What do I really want?" or "How do I want my day to unfold?" are much more useful questions.

While I'm in my Sanctuary, I ask two questions:

1. "Rita, what do you want your day to look like and how do you want to feel?"

2. "What would it take for this to happen?"

What I hear when I listen to my heart answer those questions is absolutely MAGIC! And Truth.

Every time we neglect to listen to ourselves and fill ourselves up, we steal a bit more from our creativity. And if we are stealing our creative power, then we certainly can't provide enough to share our best selves with the world.

Try asking yourself those two questions and listen, quietly and patiently, for the answers. Your heart is speaking; let it be heard. There really are no shortcuts here. Your inner voice will only speak when you allow it the opportunity. Hearing your own voice is so important in understanding what you truly want.

How will you recognize the whispers?

It's truly a whisper at first. "Why don't you try painting?" it might nudge. If you ignore it, the whisper becomes a nudge, and then that cosmic 2x4 visits. "Wake up or I am going on to someone else. Please listen to me!" The idea just feels right... like a glove that fits. You get the yummy giggles; it feels natural and so YOU.

Make the time to create this silent space. Carve out five minutes somewhere, somehow, to be still and silent. YouTube has hundreds of free meditations, from known experts, available to you right this minute. Try one of them, or just sit with yourself with no expectations. I know a woman with three small children who works full time. Before she drives home each night, she sits in her car, quietly breathing, for three to five minutes. That time is hers alone, and helps her reconnect to what's really important. Self-hugs, I call it.

You may not have a stellar breakthrough of awareness each time, but your heart, in its own way, will begin to be heard. And that's enough. It really is that simple. Please don't make it hard.

As the wonderful website Tut.com and its Notes from the Universe says:[3]

"If you sit and get really quiet, fully expecting your answer, it has to come. Guaranteed. Expectation unlocks all doors, lights all paths, and frosts all cakes."

Your part is to make the decision, the intention and do it for 21 days in a row to create the habit. Then you own it. It's a choice made from awareness. I know for certain that I handle stress MUCH better when I meditate and listen to the sounds of silence; it's where I find my whispers.

Don't steal this opportunity from yourself.

Q: Where can you find five minutes each day to fill your tank and strengthen your creative drive in life?

Rita Long with Carol Pearson

"Without the playing with fantasy no creative work has ever yet come to birth. The debt we owe to the play of imagination is incalculable."

Carl Jung

RULE #2 – JUST DO YOU

I've always been different. Always. It wasn't just feeling like I didn't fit in; it was more like not even *wanting* to fit in, knowing that the "fit" was not for me.

Dr. Wayne Dyer, one of my spiritual mentors, taught me how to honor being a "scurvy elephant." That is what he thought a teacher called him when he was young. In fact, she had actually called him a "disturbing element," but that didn't translate to his young ears. Even in his youth he questioned constantly, probing and looking for more answers; he was not like the other children.

I felt the same things – with considerably less confidence to actually express those feelings, but having them all the same. Most of us are trying to fit into our assumed tribe, craving to be accepted and liked by everyone else who matters.

Honoring your Creative Soul requires that you know who you are and acknowledge that you are worthy of love and acceptance as you are. Some of us are just learning what that means, and have to deal with 1) the fear of actually creating something, and 2) the judgment of others who will have an opinion on what we create.

Maybe you bridged that gap and just do what you want, when you want and to hell with anyone else, with no doubts or fears.

Good for you. (Share your secret with the world!) Most of us still struggle with pleasing others. Even celebrated artists, after massive phenomenal success, sometimes worry how they can top what they've already achieved – and that stops the flow of creativity dead in its tracks.

So many of the people I talk to have experienced the concept of "tribal shame," a new way of talking about a problem that is as old as humanity itself. Dr. Mario Martinez, a clinical neuropsychologist and author of "The Mind-Body Code," warns of the incredible harm that shame, and in particular tribal shaming, can do to our mental and physical health.[4]

Our tribe, he explains, is essential for human development. The idea of "it takes a village" stems from this idea as well; a connected community with similar self-interests was vital for nurturing the young, caring for the old and advancing the whole. In our modern times, the tribe has evolved to form our basic understanding of "how we do things around here," as Elizabeth Gilbert wrote in a fantastic blog post on the subject. [5]

As we grow and expand our own awareness, though, the rules of our tribe may no longer make sense. For me, some of them never made sense from the beginning. When I was a child growing up Catholic, I never believed that God would send me to hell for eating a hot dog on a Friday. It just didn't make sense for me. I understand the concept of sacrifice, but did not believe in a God that would do that if I was living a good life. I didn't expect others to follow me, or for the church to change the rules. It just didn't make sense for me.

Breaking the rules of our tribe, though, brings shame. And this kind of tribal shame can be insidious and powerful, enough to keep us from living the life we know is right for ourselves. Once we recognize that we are unique creatures, fully worthy of love, we can honor our tribe while still pursuing our own path, with compassion and love.

I have friends who are Catholic, Jewish, Democrats, Republicans (there is even a Libertarian in there), gay and straight. I am very happy it works for them. They are doing what is right for them. Likewise, paint what you love. Do what you love. Stop judging yourself and everybody else, and just do you.

As we seek to live an inspired life, filled with creativity and joy, we have to be independent of what Dr. Dyer calls "the good opinion of others." We can't give up who we are, so that others can feel better about themselves. It may work short-term, but long-term it will drain our energy and suffocate our souls

Instead, inspiration must be our master, even though following it might disappoint or confuse others. That's okay, as long as we keep our actions aligned with one foundational value: Honoring ourselves while not harming others. So you're different, so what? Are you happy? Are you able to take care of yourself and your needs? This life is not a dress rehearsal. Just Do You!

By the way, of course your idea is crazy. It's creativity knocking at your door (or your head) trying to get you to listen. Otherwise, someone else would have already done it. Think Uber, Airbnb, self-publishing a book…these ideas are not "normal," or "sane" or what the tribe expects. And that's why they so badly needed to be born. I reflect on the new way of designing living spaces in senior homes for those with Alzheimer's. The halls are made to look like streets of a small town, and the lighting is changed by the hour to mimic morning, afternoon and evening. Talk about thinking outside of the box and creating something new with meaning!

These bold new ideas would never see the light of day if the creators were so concerned with what everyone else thought. We must rise above and honor our own creative impulses.

Q: Take your 5 minutes now (longer if you want!) to quiet your mind and let this idea of "Just Do You" sink in. Then come back and jot down one little crazy idea that is bubbling inside you. Just Do You and ask yourself why you want this idea to be a reality. No judgments, no qualifying, no worries about what the tribe will think… just put the intention out there to let the idea surface, and respect the answers that come back to you.

Rita Long with Carol Pearson

"There is no innovation and creativity without failure."

Brené Brown

RULE #3 – PUT COURAGE BEFORE CONFIDENCE

The only place where confidence comes before courage is in the dictionary. Seriously.

We all want to be confident. Being confident is the coolest. Think of a time in your life when you were so confident you were giddy…you felt blissy and yummy, like you could take on the world. With that feeling of confidence you just knew you could do something, no doubt about it, bring it on! It felt good, and it was easy, because you were confident you could do it.

Doing something that you know you can do is fun. But this confidence doesn't come overnight. Getting to confident has many roads, many of them very bumpy.

I have no problem speaking in front of people; that's how I earned my living as a trainer for many years. As a beginning artist, though, in a new field that I had never played in but only dreamt about, I needed the social proof that came from people seeing my work and saying "wow, you're really good!"

That social proof increased when they asked if my paintings were for sale. Yet this kind of social proof will never happen if you never share your work with the world. Social proof can be incredibly important as we seek to gain confidence, but we have to put ourselves out there first.

"Pain pushes until the vision pulls" is how Michael Bernard Beckwith, of Agape International Spiritual Center, explained intentional creative living to Oprah recently. This is a powerful visualization to help you acknowledge and accept that there will be some pain involved as you grow into confidence in a new arena. We have to be willing to play and participate in the pain of newness; it's all part of fulfilling the creative potential. The pain is sometimes necessary to push you until your vision kicks in and pulls you. (Refer to Rule #6 – Reframe Your Beliefs for some hints on effectively dealing with this pain.)

The letting go is not always easy. Expect some rough seas. Be prepared to begin again. Let your vision grow until you no longer feel like you are being pushed outside your comfort zone, but instead feel the gentle but insistent pull of who you really are.

We are much like the leaves on the trees that emerge in the spring. They just start their journey and end up pushing away the old leaves in the process. This is the natural process of growth. If the tree is unwilling to grow, the old growth eventually smothers it and it will die. Is there old growth in your own life that might be smothering your newness?

Brené Brown in her book "Rising Strong" writes, "I want to be in the arena. I want to be brave with my life. And when we make this choice to dare greatly, we sign up to get our asses kicked. We can choose courage or we can choose comfort, but we can't have both. Not at the same time. A lot of cheap seats in the arena are filled with people who never venture onto the floor."[6]

This, to me, is an important part of creativity. We have to play and be vulnerable even when we are not confident. We need to be bold and courageous, and simply take action. Nothing else is required for now. This lesson is not a one-time deal, either. As we grow and expand, we will be continually asked to enter new arenas in which we are not confident. It's the price we have to pay, the path we follow, to get to courage.

Scott Hamilton, Olympic Gold medalist, says: "The first thing I teach my skaters at my skating academy is how to get up – because we're going to fall." He has been tested more than his share and has just received his third diagnosis of a brain tumor. His grace and joy continues as he says "I choose to celebrate life." When he told his wife, Tracie, about the tumor returning, he said "Well, here we go again." and she said, "OK, we'll just deal with it."

Think of one thing that you know you could do, right now, that would make a positive difference in building your life and your confidence. Notice I didn't say you had to be able to do it well. Pick something that will take courage and make you somewhat vulnerable. Write that article, start that blog, submit a painting to a gallery or competition, start a mastermind group so you can surround yourself with like-minded people, try that crazy difficult recipe you found and share it with your book club…it can be anything that you know takes some courage to try.

Take a deep breath and just do it. So what if no one notices? So what if you get criticized? So what if it doesn't go viral? Courage is a shortcut to confidence. There is absolutely nothing wrong with taking small, consistent steps to learn and grow and become an expert. It takes time. But if we wait around to BE confident before we try to paint, or sell our work, or live our most creative life, we are signing up for a long, lonely journey.

Bad art is the not the problem. Making no art (i.e. not being creative) is the problem.

Q: What are some of the things you know you can do to move closer toward the life you want? What scares you about doing them? Write down your thoughts below.

"To live a creative life we must call out our fear of being wrong."

Joseph Chilton Pearce

RULE #4 – CALL OUT YOUR FEAR

Fear. Fear is all around us; on social media, in the news, in the way our friends and families talk and act. We are all afraid of something. We might put different labels on it – being cautious, being conservative, taking the safe road, not wanting to rock the boat – we put different labels on it, to explain away why we don't do the things we want to do. Whatever we call it, it always ends up as fear, so let's try to understand it and make friends with it, instead of fighting it and letting it run the show.

Fear is an unpleasant, even painful, emotion caused by a belief that someone or something is dangerous, likely to cause pain, or a threat. It leads to physical symptoms that can make you miserable and make you sick. Yet researchers at the University of Cincinnati found 85% of what we worry about never happens. It's like paying interest on a loan that will never be due.

Most of the time, fear is created and coddled by us, in our minds, and grows into the thing that controls our lives.

Being a Dale Carnegie Instructor was my first real job. His book *How to Stop Worrying and Start Living*[7] is dated yet stunningly effective. One principle that he taught appears to be negative at first glance. But for many years it has helped me, and millions of others, face the truth and reality of our fear. It causes us to realistically look at the worst-case scenario. Once you do that, it often seems so ridiculous and unlikely that we actually breathe, maybe laugh, and begin to make calmer, more efficient decisions based on reality rather than fear.

The process is simple. Ask yourself, "What is the worst that can happen?"

When I decided to get a divorce, most people raised their eyebrows and did not hesitate to share their thoughts about my decision. My mother even told me that no man would ever love me as much as my husband did. Some even asked me if there was abuse (absolutely not the case) or what he had done "wrong." Fear of change can make us put labels on things and people in order to justify our decisions, even when they don't need to be justified to anyone but ourselves.

The ultimate truth in living a life that is yours alone begins with making decisions that are right for you, with no explanation needed to justify the decision to anyone else. I asked myself, "What is the worst that can happen?" Hmmm...I might be alone but I could live with that. No one was going to die because I wanted to stand in my own truth. There would be pain, but there was pain now – just a different kind. This perspective gave me the strength to look deep into my decision and the possible consequences on a different level.

This different level of understanding is so critical to growth. Albert Einstein said it well: "No problem can be solved from the same level of consciousness that created it." We have to be brave here, also. Get into the fear arena and be willing to play. Be willing to call out your fear, name it (no matter how sad or shocking) and then you can move forward.

If you ask "What's the worse that can happen?" and answer it honestly when facing your fear, you'll begin to realize that what you dread probably isn't really that bad. No one will die if you don't sell that painting. Even if you lose your job, you'll get another one; you may have to lower your standard of living for a while, but will you really starve? If you are generally a person who works hard and pays your bills, you will certainly find something else to do to keep the lights on until your dream job comes along.

If you can't live with the answer, seek some help and/or see Rule #6 – Reframe Your Beliefs for tips on dealing with the challenges of change.

Carl Jung famously said "What we resist persists." His research pointed to an interesting concept that he called "The Shadow Self." Basically he learned that if we resist certain aspects of ourselves, those aspects persist and even grow.

"This resistance typically begins with shame," explains Erol Fox in his blog The Clarity Zone.[8] "For example, a child gets called 'dumb,' feeling lots of shame. As an adult he then resists 'dumb,' striving to be smart, perfect. It becomes exhausting to run from any chance of being dumb. For example, maybe he's always wanted to write a book, but so afraid he could say something anyone would think is 'dumb,' so he never writes, ever. The more he resists, the more the pain persists. Oddly, he'll be plagued by random occasions of really 'dumb' things, more shames, more striving for perfection."

For the creative person, the resistance might start with believing you don't have enough time or talent to do your art, rather than not being smart enough.

As I've grown as an artist, I've come up with my own process for dealing with the fear that inevitably creeps in.

1. It starts with naming your fear: I call it out as False Evidence Appearing Real. What is it that you're really afraid of? Dig deep and name it. It's never about not having the time; there's always something deeper.

2. Make friends with your fear. Don't ignore it. Acknowledge its presence, talk to it, but let it know in no uncertain terms that it is no longer in control.

3. Then, take action. Do something, get moving, call someone, paint something, start a project you've been putting off, buy that pair of shoes. If you consistently address your fear instead of pretending it's not there, amazing things will begin to happen. It's magic. Action is the magical antidote to fear.

Q: Take a few minutes now and ask yourself "what am I really afraid of?" Write it down; spell it out. Then reread what you wrote and ask yourself "What's the worst that can happen?" You might be surprised how much lighter you feel.

Rita Long with Carol Pearson

"Keep away from people who try to belittle your ambitions. Small people always do that, but the really great make you feel that you too, can become great. When you are seeking to bring big plans to fruition, it is important with whom you regularly associate. Hang out with friends who are like-minded and who are also designing purpose-filled lives. Similarly be that kind of a friend for your friends."

Mark Twain

RULE # 5 – SURROUND YOURSELF

During a challenging time many years ago when my son was in high school, I remember telling him to be aware of the friends he was choosing. "Be careful who you hang out with, son."

The same warning holds true for all of us. Be very careful when you choose your friends and associates. It's said that we become like the five people with whom we spend the most time. Interesting to consider, isn't it?

If we find we are becoming more negative, maybe one of those closest to us is talking negatively. Or maybe we watch the news night and day, "hanging out" with the on-air celebrities that substitute for trusted friends. The news, on a side note, is relentlessly negative; you might want to take a break from it for a week and see how you feel.

I was shopping yesterday and, while waiting in line to check out, overheard four different conversations about other people's bad decisions and actions. Some of these conversations were one-sided on the phone; the others were between people standing in line together. Luckily I didn't know any of these people personally, so I could choose not to participate or hang out with them in the future. When I am among people I know, I often try to guide negative conversations onto a more neutral or positive topic.

We all have days when we want to let off steam about things, or people, or the weather, or the boss; it's human nature to need a place to vent, and a good friend can be a safe place for that. But some people engage in this negativity all the time. Short-term it can be tolerated, but as a way of life? No thank you.

Who are you with most often? Do you truly enjoy their company? Do they draw you into criticism and judgement, or talk about goals, dreams and positive things?

Personally – and it is a personal choice – I strive to surround myself with big thinkers, people who are decisive, embrace change, are interested in growth and learning, are bright and kind. My favorite kinds of people are proactive, spontaneous, fun, enthusiastic, positive, connected, with an abundance mindset and true leadership qualities. And I like to hang with people who look for solutions instead of problems.

In the movie "Jerry McGuire," Tom Cruise's title character asks Renee Zellweger's character Dorothy why she chose to follow him into his new, risky adventure. She simply replied, "I want to be inspired." Be on the lookout for people who inspire you. Like Dorothy, aim to include dreamers, visionaries, and courageous decision-makers into your life. Look for people who inspire you and do what you can to spend time with them!

Inspiration is critical to the creative process, and it often comes from the people we share space with. Likewise, negativity is a creativity killer.

We all have negative people in our lives, some by choice and some by design. Some we can limit, and some – due to family, work or life situations – we are basically stuck with. But we do have choices – even when it comes to our families. Set your boundaries and insist on respectful behavior; if that doesn't work, try for fewer or shorter visits. If you prefer a gentler approach, positive change can start with your own awareness. Pay attention to the conversations you are in and, if they start to take a negative turn, don't add to it. Attempt to steer the conversation in a more positive direction, or ask probing questions about why the negative person feels a certain way. Be careful not to be judgmental in your response; that's just another form a negative thinking. Remember from Rule #3, we talked about moving toward the life you want to live, asking:

"What do you want your day to look like and how do you want to feel?"

"What would it take for this to happen?"

These questions will change how you move forward; they are pivotal in helping you understanding not just your own thinking, but how the people surrounding you could be influencing your success (or your stuckness!).

This approach really can change the tenor of your relationships. You may get some strange looks at first (it can be kind of fun if you take the right approach) but eventually they'll get the message and realize that being negative around you isn't as much fun as it used to be.

On the flip side of this coin lie your own actions. Do you actively support the big dreams and juicy goals of those closest to you? Do you bask in their accomplishments, without jealousy? Do you help them with your support, your connections, and your own positive energy?

I guarantee you that if you make a commitment to doing this, you will find miraculous things begin to happen. Not only will many of the people in your life become more positive, you'll also attract new people to you who share your sunny vibe.

Q: Who are the five or six people you are around most often? Do they inspire you and lift you up? Take a few minutes here to jot down some ideas for how you can avoid being caught up in any negativity or useless drama. Also take a look at your own behavior, and commit to being more aware of any possibly negative tendencies. Instead, be more excited about being a positive voice.

"Write the bad things that are done to you in the sand, but write the good things that happen to you on a piece of marble."

Arabic Parable

RULE # 6 – REFRAME YOUR BELIEFS …
IN SAND OR IN MARBLE

How do we manage our experiences and memories? Do we carry around beliefs about our past that may not be true? And how does this limit our creative expression in the moment?

This idea of our beliefs is so important because what we perceive, believe and tell ourselves is not necessarily in tune with reality. And while it may not be reality, it is still *our truth* and *our reality*, until we take steps to reframe our beliefs.

Last summer I was talking to an amazing artist who had just spoken to a group of artists about his latest work. After his talk, I sought him out to compliment him on his many recent awards and his astonishing talent. (Really, his artwork is just incredible…so detailed and precise, and dripping with emotion.) The conversation swirled downward as he talked about how much time and effort he put into his pieces and then about the potential customers who wouldn't pay the price he was asking.

"My customers determine what my work is worth," he stated flatly.

In truth, he should be getting 1,000 times more for his work than what he was charging, but he believes his own story that his work is only worth what his customers will pay. If he believes this story as truth, he has little control in creating what he really wants. If he reframes his story, *believing in his mind and in his core that there are people out there who will buy his work at the right price*, it changes everything.

When we can integrate these new beliefs, resentment disappears and we start to attract the "right" customers who value our work and are happy to pay our price.

Some beliefs we have may just be the story we are telling ourselves. We tell it often enough and that story becomes real to us. Other beliefs may have been put there by our tribe. "That's not the way we do things" can easily become "I can't do that" if we hear it often enough.

We all have our story. We all tell ourselves that story, over and over again. and it does nothing but stand in the way of our true creative selves. The solution? Make up a new story. Yes, you can do that and you must do that if you want your life to expand.

The frames I put on my original paintings and prints completely change not only the look, but the emotions and the value of each piece. And when I tell the story behind that painting, how it came to be, it seems to be more popular and increases in value with my customers. They love the "frames" I put around their paintings, both literal and figurative.

If you are feeling stuck, it's time to reframe your story.

You can write your stories in either sand, or in marble, as the parable goes. For every perceived or real failure, you can take the negative to heart by writing it in marble, or simply acknowledge it and then let it go by writing it in the sand. The marble is permanent, while the sand can be washed away.

If you have made a mistake, learn from it, write it in sand (you can do this in your imagination if you don't live by the sea), and let it go. Get your mental marker out and create a new, empowering story with juicy and joyous details. Make it the movie of your life and make yourself the star.

When a customer commissions me to do a painting, their request bubbles up from a cherished memory of a special moment or time. The painting, or mural, captures those memories permanently. This makes sense with good experiences; we get to relive them through the artwork every time we see the piece. Would you commission a permanent piece of art that continually reminded you of a negative memory or limiting experience? Of course not. Yet that's what we do every time we internalize criticism, self-doubt or failure. We write it in marble.

This idea really resonated with the brilliant Sandi Maki of The InSights Group. "I love it," she said. "It's amazing to think of ocean waves washing away the bad things that you just don't want. You don't even have to physically write in the sand, just image it. Sit back and watch the waves erase it. It's gone. It's like it never happened."

When you can do this, you realize you don't have to carry this sad old story with you any longer. You can let it go! The beach and the water are not hurt by it; they don't even notice what they are erasing. What you wrote in the sand is nothing more than a bird's footprint. The energy of the ocean is not changed by you or what happened to you or the words that it consumed.

If someone is not willing to pay what your work is worth, they simply are not the right customer. The art does not speak to them. That's okay. Write the idea that your art "isn't worth it" in sand, and let it be erased. Scott Hamilton may not be able to erase the tumor diagnosis, but he sure is reframing how he deals with it.

What this reframing does to you is nothing short of stunning. As we watch the waves erase those old beliefs, and see them disappear…wow. Ahhhh, doesn't that feel better?

When the old ideas are washed away, it's time to carve your new story in marble. Know your worth as a creative being, and honor that knowing with a solid new story of light, love and creativity. Begin now to create your own beliefs about yourself, your value and your work. Remember that you, and no one else, is the Artist, the Director and the Decision Maker for your life.

Q: What beliefs about your creative journey hold you back? Where are you struggling to move forward, and what beliefs are getting in the way? Write down whatever comes to mind, then close your eyes, picture yourself writing them in the sand, and sit on the beach and let the waves quietly wash them away.

Rita Long with Carol Pearson

"When you know that you are in charge of your intentions, then you will come to know that you are in charge of your entire world."

Dr. Wayne Dyer

RULE # 7 – BE "FOR" SOMETHING

It's a phenomenon of being human that whatever we focus on expands in our awareness. A couple thinking of having a child suddenly see pregnant women everywhere they look.

We notice this idea in the news every day. Our "war on drugs" seems to make the problem worse. Our war on terror turns into more and more horrible attacks. Our social outcry over human rights abuse seems to be overshadowed by reports every day of more atrocities. We can all feel so helpless.

Yet it doesn't have to be this way. Being against drugs, poverty and human trafficking isn't nearly as effective as being *for* an enlightened, educated youth; a higher standard of living for all; and respect for everyone's rights and dignity. Remember – whatever we focus on expands. Focus on what you are *for*: what you love, what you want, what you know, who you want to see in your life, where you see yourself living and traveling, how you feel, and what kind of world you want to experience.

The same truth applies to the things you create. Art speaks to people on an emotional level, in large part because of the energy and intention the artist puts into it. If it doesn't resonate, that person won't like it and won't buy it… and that's OK. Your role as an artist is to understand that your work carries meaning. Creativity is an active endeavor, and it's important to understand why you do what you do. In other words, it's important to know why you create, and what positive change you are hoping your art makes...in the buyer, or in the world at large.

Not knowing your "why" can lead to indecision. As an artist you may hesitate and have a tendency to hold back for fear (there's that word again) you might offend someone or make waves. That hesitancy will show up everywhere in your life, including in your ability to create.

How can we be creative and let our light shine if we are holding back and hesitant? To truly embrace our creative potential, we must take the time and energy to understand and acknowledge our "why."

A great place to start is Simon Sinek's incredible book "Start With Why."[9] Knowing and embracing your "why" makes all your future decisions so much easier.

What is your intention in your creative work? What do you want to focus on? We have to remember that art needs to be emotional for the artist, too. Paint what you love, tell a story that lifts you up, be "for" something rather than against it. This is the path of true connection between the creator and the people who will choose to associate with what you create.

One of my greatest inspirations is artist and storyteller Pamela Alderman.[10] In 2014, at the Art Prize in Grand Rapids, Michigan, I was transformed forever while walking through a 40-foot storage container that told a story of healing. Her installation "The Scarlet Cord" aired the truth about a secret, dark world, but her art ultimately is the story of healing. Rather than focus on the darkness itself, she focuses on the healing and the light that comes from it.

My art is not so profound; I have no broad social injustice I'm working to resolve. It does for my clients what a Jimmy Buffett concert does for his Parrotheads. I call my paintings "Vacations in a Frame." I also create permanent reminders of "Moments That Matter" from their lives. It's not as noble maybe as the work of a statesman or others, but folks seem to smile and remember the best parts of their lives and dreams when they connect with one of my pieces.

My "why" is to inspire people to express themselves and do what matters most to them ... in whatever form that may take. Painting is one of the ways I express myself and my purpose; but it's not my only way. Everything I do reflects a willingness to know myself and express who I am, and to encourage others to do the same. That is my intention, my why. That is what I am *for*.

As I am writing this, it is an election year here in the United States. As the day to vote gets closer, the social media comments, commercials, talk shows and even entertainment programs focus more on what they don't want, can't live with and dislike about all of the candidates. Rarely do we see or hear why we are "for" one or the other. What we focus on becomes our reality. As we focus on the negatives around our choices, more negativity follows. Our thoughts become things, so be very careful what you think about.

Al Curtis, "Ask The Pool Guy" of Legendary Escapes, is a perfect example of someone who understands this rule and applies it routinely. Al only speaks of the candidate he favors, never mentioning the one he doesn't want. There is no bashing or complaining; he simply states how wonderful it will be when his candidate wins the election.

We do have a choice. If you are going to accept responsibility for writing the script for your life, be steadfast in your efforts to cast yourself as the star! And make sure the other actors and crew can see you as a living example of your beliefs, your life and your story.

I now live by intention; my life is driven by what I am *for*, what I want to see and feel in my life, by the good energy of the people with whom I choose to spend my time…and always by what gives me the yummy giggles inside.

My intention is simply to live a passionate, joyful and healthy life.

Q: What are you for? What lights you up and makes you long to share with others? Take some time to reflect on this, writing down your answers. Then go do more of that, with the clear intention of your "why" behind it. This is the key to beginning to build a creative and artful life that resonates with your soul and helps define your place in the Universe.

Rita Long with Carol Pearson

"Please take responsibility for the energy you bring into this space."

Dr. Jill Bolte Taylor

RULE #8 – UNDERSTAND YOUR ENERGY SIGNATURE

A therapist in one of my classes once gave me spot-on advice about relationships and the people and circumstances we attract into our lives.

All humans either give you energy or take it from you, he said, and it's our job to notice.

We all have ups and downs, good days and bad. No one is 100 percent up all the time. But beneath the ebbs and flows is one constant: our Energy Signature. It's the overall vibration that we put out into the world. And that vibration has everything to do with what we get back.

Energy is everything, and everything is energy.

Our energy signature is our heartbeat. People feel it whether we speak or not, because it runs through our walk, our demeanor, our comments, our writing and yes, the things we create.

What do you get when you squeeze an orange? Orange juice! Why do we get orange juice when we squeeze an orange? Because that's what is inside. We can pretend we'll get something else, but we can't fake it for very long. The truth of what's inside always makes itself known eventually.

If we are creative in nature rather than competitive, that energy will shine out of our very pores.

If we believe in the power of connection rather than "it's a dog-eat-dog world," we vibrate and attract like-minded people, people who want to help us succeed and celebrate our victories.

If we believe that thoughts become things, rather than believing that it's out of our control and it's useless to try, we understand our essential nature as creative beings and artistic souls.

Your energy runs through everything you do, including what you create. It says who you are without a spoken word. People see it, feel it, and respond in some way and are either drawn toward you or pushed way.

Think about times when you have to use your signature on a legal paper, or on your art. It's you, your word, your promise, your whole being. You are proud to sign it and own it. You are making a statement that says "Yes, I choose this, I make this decision, this is who I am and what I want, and this is how I think and what I believe." Your signature is binding and uniquely yours. It represents who you are.

Years ago, an intruder broke into my home where my 19-year-old daughter and I were sleeping. As I came out of my bedroom and walked toward her room, she came into the hallway and announced that he had been in her room when she awoke. We looked to the end of the hallway and there he stood. Without a word, we turned toward him, our shoulders touched and we, together and without a word, forced him out the door. It was probably not a very smart thing to do but I remember to this day the pure energy signature we sent to him.

Last week, I was painting and everything suddenly started to go badly. The colors weren't right; I was making mistakes and getting upset. Typically, I am in the FLOW when I paint so this was unusual. I stopped and asked myself what was going on. Upon reflection, I had been having an unpleasant conversation (in my mind) with someone I had met with earlier. Bam! Right from my monkey mind onto my canvas… instantly. The energy was totally there and flowing through me, without me realizing it.

This energy actually travels through the material things that we create and share. Everything is energy. I participated as a vendor at a Ladies Night and decided to give something away to each visitor regardless of whether they bought any of my artwork or not. So I went online and purchased 200 pens that actually looked like a paint brush! I chose a good quality pen that wrote well, and added my Rita Long Art logo to the handle. People were coming up to my table asking for one of those paint brush pens like it was worth hundreds of dollars. They could not believe I was giving away something so unique and of such high quality! I believe I put my Energy Signature into that gift, representing me and my art, with all my best self-expression, attention to quality, creativity, sharing and fun. It was this energy – not the value of the actual pen itself – that I believe they felt that night. I know they will remember me and I believe it will be in the best way possible.

Remember, we want people to be happy when we arrive, not when we leave the room!

Our energy shows up whether we intend it to or not, and it usually makes itself known before our spoken words come out of our mouths. "I like this ... I don't like this ... I feel slighted ... I feel appreciated ... I don't want to be here ... why am I doing this?" Whatever is going on inside can be felt by those who are perceptive enough to realize it. Energy holds space, in our emotions and in our physical world. Yours has the power to impact everything around you.

Q: What do people feel when you walk into a room? What do you want them to feel when you leave? What is your Energy Signature? It's really your calling card! Do you think your energy signature is drawing in the right people and circumstances, or keeping them out? Give this some thought and write down your answers. What kind of energy signature would you need in order to attract the things you want in your life?

Rita Long with Carol Pearson

"The essence of all beautiful art,
all great art, is gratitude."

Friedrich Nietzsche

RULE # 9 – BE GRATEFUL

One lovely December night many years ago, I found myself on a boat, with coworkers from a project, motoring out to see the Statue of Liberty. We went right up to her and saw her lights gleaming, welcoming all. Later, we went on a private tour of Manhattan to see the city's Christmas decorations ... Times Square and that huge tree decorated with millions of lights. What a sight!

I remember how my sister pulled me to my senses and set me straight that night. I was on the phone with her, complaining about how tired I was from working all day, and it was chilly on the boat, and .... well, you get the idea.

She said, "Rita, for heaven's sake, do you know how many people would love to be where you are right now? I've never seen the Statue of Liberty, or done any of the things you are doing right now. Be grateful! Be thankful! It's a blessing; enjoy it!"

How true that was. And it brought me up short, to realize that I was complaining about this really incredible experience.

In "10 Little Rules for a Blissy Life," Carol Pearson writes about the transforming power of gratitude in her own life.

"One of the most challenging aspects of gratitude is being

grateful during the tough times. Last December I found myself in the emergency room with a post-surgery complication, feeling scared and horribly sick. I forced myself to find things to be grateful for: the good medical care I was about to receive; the loving and concerned husband sitting next to me; even the fact that the little girl carried in by her dad was going to be seen before me," she writes.[11]

In the very act of acknowledging the good, we have the power to lessen the bad. Every day I try to remind myself to be grateful for what I have. It does not mean I don't have goals or I've given up and will settle for what I've got. Rather it means I have an understanding of life's smallest gifts.

Every time I get in my car I say, "Thank you for all the safe trips you've given us and please help us have a safe trip today."

I have been involved in two serious car accidents, so I truly appreciate every car ride I've taken without incident. Instead of being fearful of traveling, I focus on what I want (a safe car ride) and express gratitude. I also declared one day that I was NOT going to have another accident. So far so good.

I'm proud to say that now the grandchildren automatically say it every time we get in the car, without prompting.

Being grateful is a show-stopper. It's a game-changer and a life-changer. It changes energy. It brings in more to be thankful for and starts a cycle of hope. And with hope all things are possible.

Marelisa Fabrega, author of The Change Blog, writes about Gratitude in her post "How Gratitude Can Change Your Life," and cites research on gratitude that proves its power to transform.[12]

"One of the things these studies show is that practicing gratitude can increase happiness levels by around 25%. This is significant, among other things, because just as there's a certain weight that feels natural to your body and which your body strives to maintain, your basic level of happiness is set at a predetermined point. If something bad happens to you during the day, your happiness can drop momentarily, but then it returns to its natural set-point. Likewise, if something positive happens to you, your level of happiness rises, and then it returns once again to your "happiness set-point". A practice of gratitude raises your 'happiness set-point' so you can remain at a higher level of happiness regardless of outside circumstances.

"In addition...research shows that those who practice gratitude tend to be more creative, bounce back more quickly from adversity, have a stronger immune system, and have stronger social relationships than those who don't practice gratitude. He further points out that "To say we feel grateful is not to say that everything in our lives is necessarily great. It just means we are aware of our blessings."

Gratitude and Energy can create empires! I'm a Parrothead; I just love Jimmy Buffett. Not only is he a fantastic story-teller, performer and band leader (maybe not the best singer in the world), but after nearly 40 years in the business and phenomenal success, he thanks his audiences at every performance for allowing him to do the job he loves. It never fails; he always say "thank you" at his concerts.

A huge part of his success comes down to the platform he's

created by simply being grateful. The fans feel it in his music, and it draws them in every time. His Energy Signature is also there; can you feel it? You not only feel it, you can put it into words. Jimmy's a master at creating energy and being grateful.

Notice and appreciate every "small" gift of each day. I am thankful for indoor plumbing! Think about it; I'm serious!

Dale Carnegie's very first rule in "How to Win Friends and Influence People" is Do Not Criticize, Condemn or Complain. I often included this idea as part of my corporate trainings.

I would give each class member a 3x5 card to carry with them for 24 hours. Their assignment was to jot down each and every time they criticized, condemned or complained about anything or anyone, including themselves. They came back the next week and some had added 10 to 20 more cards that itemized their previously unnoticed judgments and thoughts, both spoken and unspoken.

Some were in tears realizing the extent of their own negativity, and others spoke about how coworkers and family members seemed so much happier now that the negativity was noticed and in better check. It really does work from the inside out, doesn't it?

Try noticing your own negativity for a day or two; you might be stunned to realize how often you go there. Then, train yourself to be grateful instead of negative, and see how your world changes. As we step into our most creative lives, gratitude is what will help get us there faster. Gratitude is a short-cut to success and bliss.

Q: Take some time now and reflect on a recent challenging or upsetting experience. Try to look at it through the lens of gratitude. Who was there to help? What good things happened in the course of your going through the challenge? What kind words were said, or help offered? Write down what you remember, and give thanks.

Rita Long with Carol Pearson

"Just don't give up trying to do what you really want to do. Where there is love and inspiration, I don't think you can go wrong."

Ella Fitzgerald

RULE # 10 – STOP IT!

Is it your turn to start living a more creative existence? Or have you decided you can't do that because:

You're too young…

You're too old…

Your resume is thin…

Who do you think you are, anyway?

You can't just do that without years of effort…

You don't know the right people…

People won't pay you what it's worth…

No one has done that before…

People have said *no* to you…

No one will help you…

Please. Just Stop It.

These are only stories that you are telling yourself, and you can change the story right now.

Think of your mind like your computer or smartphone. There is a delete button on those gadgets for a reason; it gets rid of the junk. So use it when you catch yourself doubting, making excuses, refusing to face your fear (re-read Rules #4 – Call Out Your Fear, and #5 – Surround Yourself), being lazy or complacent, or thinking about things you really don't want.

Try the "What If" experiment sometime. What if you did this thing without expecting any specific outcome? What if you did it just because you wanted to try it? What if it works? What if you don't like it? "What If" is a great question and can give us valuable feedback. The bottom line is whether or not YOU want to do it and whether or not it FEELS GOOD and NATURAL to you.

Recently I ordered 130 glass Christmas tree ornaments to paint, along with the fancy boxes and ribbons to package the beauties for delivery to my many customers who wanted them. The more I got into the project, the more I started listening to my inner knower, which was telling me "no." But I pushed through and finally cleared my schedule to begin the Bulb Brigade!

And I came up against a wall. It just wasn't happening. I felt the pressure, pain and pointlessness of doing something I so obviously don't want to do. So I said "STOP IT". And I did. And I felt better immediately. My creativity since that time has exploded because I am doing what makes me happy, not what I "should" do.

The "stop it" technique works both ways. If we are making excuses for *not* doing something, we can remind ourselves to stop it and look for different ways to move our creative projects ahead. Or, if we are in the midst of something and just know that it's not the right approach (like the Christmas bulb project), we can make the decision to stop. It's all about being aware of those inner voices and creative urges.

But what about all those bulbs? My next Paint Party Project is ready and those students are going to love creating their own unique Christmas ornament. And I'll donate any leftovers to a local senior center. What matters is respecting the whispers inside me, and knowing when it's not right.

What do you want and why do you want it? If you have clarity and can see it, feel it, and have faith… it's already yours. Open your arms and receive it.

Act, move, make a decision…take that first step and your world will change.

One great way to get started is by reading any of these books. Just pick one that appeals to you and start it; don't overthink it. You can't make a wrong decision here.

• "Choose Yourself: Be Happy, Make Millions, Live the Dream" by James Altucher

• "What To Do When It's Your Turn (and it's always your turn)" by Seth Godin

• Anything written by Dr. Wayne Dyer

• "Steal Like an Artist: 10 Things Nobody Told You About Being Creative" or "Show Your Work: 10 Ways to Share Your Creativity and Get Discovered" by Austin Kleon

• "The Artist's Way: A Spiritual Path the Higher Creativity" by Julia Cameron

The great thing about living in today's world is the speed with which we can access information.

Go to YouTube and learn anything. Google a topic that interests you and find a blog to read. Better yet, start blogging yourself. Begin to tell your story and put yourself out there.

Ultimately, you want to keep choosing yourself and being creative until your creative soul can no longer be ignored.

Q: What's holding you back? What do you need to stop doing, thinking or saying to have the creative life you long to live? Write down your commitment to getting past it, getting over, and just stopping the resistance to your creative instincts. This is for you – no one else – and you are about to take ownership in a way you never have before. Stop holding yourself back and start to live – creatively, abundantly and fearlessly. What do you commit to do, or stop doing, to move into your most creative life? Commit it to paper here.

Rita Long with Carol Pearson

She let go. Without a thought or a word, she let go.

She let go of the fear. She let go of the judgments. She let go of the confluence of opinions swarming around her head. She let go of the committee of indecision within her. She let go of all the 'right' reasons. Wholly and completely, without hesitation or worry, she just let go.

She didn't ask anyone for advice. She didn't read a book on how to let go. She didn't search the scriptures. She just let go. She let go of all of the memories that held her back. She let go of all of the anxiety that kept her from moving forward. She let go of the planning and all of the calculations about how to do it just right.

She didn't promise to let go. She didn't journal about it. She didn't write the projected date in her Day-Timer. She made no public announcement and put no ad in the paper. She didn't check the weather report or read her daily horoscope. She just let go.

She didn't analyze whether she should let go. She didn't call her friends to discuss the matter. She didn't do a five-step Spiritual Mind Treatment. She didn't call the prayer line. She didn't utter one word. She just let go.

No one was around when it happened. There was no applause or congratulations. No one thanked her or praised her. No one noticed a thing. Like a leaf falling from a tree, she just let go.

There was no effort. There was no struggle. It wasn't good and it wasn't bad. It was what it was, and it is just that.

In the space of letting go, she let it all be. A small smile came over her face. A light breeze blew through her. And the sun and the moon shone forevermore.

~ Rev. Safire Rose, via Lightworkers World

Rita Long with Carol Pearson

Stay connected to
the 10 Little Rules Community

Visit our site at www.10littlerules.com

Books in the *10 Little Rules* series:

10 Little Rules for a Blissy Life by Carol Pearson

10 Little Rules for Your Creative Soul by Rita Long with Carol Pearson

10 Little Rules for Hank: A family's journey through a rare disease by Wendy Price with Carol Pearson (January 2017)

10 Little Rules for Moms and Daughters by Beverly Ingle with Carol Pearson (Spring 2017)

Join our Facebook page for ongoing support and discussion on how to apply these books to living your best life:

www.facebook.com/10littlerules

Rita Long with Carol Pearson

ABOUT THE AUTHORS

Rita Long is the talented artist behind Rita Long Art and her "Memories that Matter" paintings. Not only is her artwork gorgeous, she also has a solid corporate training background and uses that to help other artists expand their creative efforts and their businesses. She is the author of *10 Little Rules for Your Creative Soul*, a book that will help your creative spark burst into full flame. View her work at www.ritalongart.com.

Carol Pearson is a ghostwriter and wordsmith (they call her The Words Girl), a business marketing strategist and the creator of the original *10 Little Rules for a Blissy Life*. When she's not writing, she's editing her garden (some call it weeding), traveling or moving mountains for the people she loves. Visit her site at www.thewordsgirl.com.

END NOTES

[1] Novoteny, Amy. (2016). "The science of creativity." American Psychological Association. Retrieved on October 5, 2016 from www.apa.org.

[2] Canfield, Jack. (2016) "7 Steps to Strengthen Your Intuition and Take Soul-Inspired Action." Retrieved on October 5, 2016 from www.jackcanfield.com.

[3] "Notes from the Universe" daily email inspirations, accessed on October 11, 2016. www.tut.com.

[4] Martinez, Mario, PsyD. (2014). "The MindBody Code: How to Change the Beliefs that Limit Your Health, Longevity, and Success." Sounds True Publishing.

[5] Gilbert, Elizabeth. (2015) "Beware of Tribal Shame." Retrieved October 6, 2016 on www.facebook.com

[6] Brown, Brené. (2015). Rising Strong: The Reckoning. The Rumble. The Revolution. Speigel & Grau.

[7] Carnegie, Dale. (1984). *How to Stop Worry and Start Living*. Simon & Schuster.

[8] Fox, Erol. (2010). "What you resist persist. What did Jung really mean by this?" Retrieved on October 12, 2016 at www.clarity.zone.

[9] Sinek, Simon. (2009). "Start with Why: How Great Leaders Inspire Everyone to Take Action." Portfolio Publishing.

[10] Alderman, Pamela. (2016). "The Scarlet Cord Showcases at the Kent County Courthouse." Accessed on October 17, 2016 on www.pamelaalderman.com.

11] Pearson, Carol. (2016) "10 Little Rules for a Blissy Life." Skydog Creations LLC.

[12] Fabrega, Marelisa. (2008). "How Gratitude Can Change Your Life." Accessed on November 9, 2016 on www.thechangeblog.com.

Rita Long with Carol Pearson

Made in the USA
San Bernardino, CA
13 January 2017